CW00420619

That Curious Love of Green

Notes From a Writer's Journal

Jane Gilheaney Barry

Copyright © 2019 Jane Gilheaney Barry
All rights reserved. No part of this book may be reproduced,
scanned, or redistributed in any printed or electronic form
without prior, written permission of the author.

Dedication

To my girls, Shaylyn, Saoirse & Sadhbh

Acknowledgements

Thanks to my wonderful husband Adrian whose big idea this little book was. For always supporting me, and for taking the beautiful cover photo. Thanks also to my brilliant editor Sheryl and cover designer Mirna. And to my early readers Kim, Aisling, Martha, Kay, and Nicola. I couldn't have had a better team of people around me. Finally, I want to thank my readers and followers at That Curious Love of Green. Some of you have been with me from the start of this journey. Thank you for your generous support, love and encouragement this past seven years.

Pronunciation Guide

Shaylyn – 'Shay-lyn' – Derived from old Irish. Meaning 'From the fairy-fort.'

Saoirse – 'Sayr-sha' – Irish/Gaelic. Meaning 'Freedom.'

Sadhbh – Rhymes with five. 'Sigh-iv' – Meaning 'Lovely, sweet, good.'

Contents

Introduction

For thirty-nine years I was one of those people who know they're not living their creative potential. It's a half-life for people like me. I was at home for the first time too, with a toddler, a baby, a teen, little means, not driving, and no place to go if I did, in two of the worst winters in Irish living memory. I was also still suffering the effects of medical traumas that had really crushed my 'ness.' To quote the Mad Hatter;

'You used to be much muchier, you've lost your muchness.'

That was me. But I was determined to get it back. I knew I wanted to write, to paint, and have a freer more creatively fulfilled existence. I just didn't know how to get it. So I started a blog. I hadn't written creatively in over 20 years but within a year of regular, open-hearted blogging, I started writing a novel.

In September 2018 I published *Cailleach~Witch*, a modern gothic mystery about a family of outsider women. I'm currently working on two more in that series *Banshee* and *Changeling* – The Story of Ellen Cleary. Meanwhile, this little book is the first in a series too, a series of non-fiction books (cookbook and creativity books coming next!) based on *That Curious Love of Green*, the blog that started it all.

That Curious Love of Green stands for creativity, creative courage, and the individual. To support and encourage creativity. We don't live in that kind of world, but we can create it. That's something I aim to do. Create my own world and empower the creative spirit that lives in us all.

I'm lucky I now get to spend my days writing, creating, seeking inspiration, doing the kind of work I always wanted to do, living the kind of life I always wanted to live. It's not easy, but it is for me. The landscape of Co. Leitrim, in the north west of Ireland where I grew up is a deep well of inspiration. It is the soul of my writing. Something in the landscape here, along with writing, saved me.

One of the things fans of *Cailleach* said they loved most was the sense of place, seasons, and the elements. They said the natural world felt like *another character*. This book, written while I was writing *Cailleach*, goes a way to explaining that. A book inside a book if you will. I never thought of it being published in its own right. And yet here it is.

My hope is it offers some measure of comfort and inspiration for the creative spirit. I hope it encourages someone to take up the pen and start writing. To reach for their own creative dreams, and make them happen.

With Love, Jane.

2013

1. *Blustery* (March)

I prefer a wild night to a silent night,
waves to a smooth sea,
clouds to a clear sky,
snow as it's falling,
and the wind more than anything.
Especially when it's blustery.

2. *May*

Afternoon already, another morning gone like so much sand through my fingers, and what have I to show for it?

Yesterday I read the first six chapters of my book for the first time in a long time and knew that when this *'most intensive edit yet'* is finished, I'm going to have to start again, another edit.

I'm just letting that sink in. Meanwhile, grey May continues.

Outside is wet, warm and woodsmoke.

Azaleas,

mock orange,

lilac and rose bushes doubled in size,

even the oak trees we planted have budded.

This means all the trees, all sixty we planted,

survived.

I think,

I think if I could just climb up into the sky and pull

those clouds back,

if I could just finish my book.

But then I go outside and look at the trees and know,

it's grey,

but it is still May.

3. *July is Flowing By*

July is flowing by,

all drip, no dry,

and the mood has shifted, did you feel it? The

collective sigh.

And the sigh said,

it's late now for rallying cries for blue skies.

July is flowing up,

up from the green earth,

over the people's hopes,

reflected in birds' eyes,

down from the grey skies,

swelling the water supply.

July is flowing by,

I think I'll flow with it.

4. Sadhbh's Reasons at 2.00 a.m. For Not Sleeping

'I want to sleep with Daddy.
I want to dance.
There's a monkey at my toe.'

5. Girls Yis Are Lookin Alright (August)

When you go to Dublin from Leitrim the shift starts at
the station,
with a single step from green to stone.
Under the arch at Dromad station, generations
passed,
green at their backs for the first and last time.
Most of them never returned.
You feel that more in stones than grass.

The train emptied at Drumcondra for the match.
The stream of jerseys, rising banter and brollies
spilled as far as the eye could see,
beyond the platform,

down on the roads,

under the ancient trees.

I had the train to myself for the heave into Connolly.

There's a stunning lake view from the Sligo/Dublin train,

but my favourite is the view of the houses in the city.

Array of disarray, spellbinding,

Stories being told, new stories and old.

From the station to O'Connell Bridge I weave along familiar roads and pavements.

The clock turns back.

Here's the building where and there's the corner that.

The air is full of brewing hops and memory.

I take out across O'Connell Bridge, and hesitate as cars take flight,

where I once ran young and full of light.

That old young feeling.

And a day coming home in the setting sun,

when I gazed down the curve of the Liffey,

at the buildings turning fiery red,

comes back to me.

Bewley's on D'olier Street's now a Starbucks, is that even legal?

God it's horrible.

Trinity holds its magic still.

I glance in as I pass, and feel the ghosts, of those inside,

from Ernie O'Malley to Oscar Wilde.

Nobody waits for the traffic lights.

We rush on lyrically.

You hear all the chat, and the half chat, and many things that make you laugh.

All comes to a halt at the Molly Malone where a leprechaun's posing for photographs.

On Grafton Street the pace slows down for music, art, and giant bubbles.

'Can we just set up and play?'

'I don't know, are ye any good?' says the guard.

The council's digging up the old pink bricks, laying a new and ugly grey that people aren't happy with.

There's been complaining but it's going.

At Bewley's there's always a breeze or in winter a gale as you push the doors in, and the scent of fresh coffee could knock you back again. The dark wood's transporting, evocative, welcoming.

I love the blue room and the street sounds coming up,

sea breezes in the windows,

how the sun rests on the building tops.

That night in Rathmines we went dancing,

and coming home we walked behind a drunk guy.

When he stopped to talk to friends he said we'd been following him all night.

'What are yis laughin at!' he cried.

Jane Gilheaney Barry

Martha lives near Palmerston Park,

behind a yellow door with a fan light.

Her room is all window to seagull skies,

magnolia trees, city for miles.

Always in Dublin you're walking, and if you're me,

avoiding pigeons.

We're still busy talking when comes the refrain,

'Any spare change? It's my throat, has me up all

night.'

As we pass he says, 'Girls, yis are looking alright.'

6. Imprints

With each new day comes new hope and regret,

regret for the morning,

knowing I won't remember it,

hope for the words I might write yet.

I'll linger and savour,

my wish,

to recall it forever.

See the flowers linger too this fair October,

but it can't last.

Soon I'll stand here shivering in the biting winds of winter,

one day, with the flowers, I'll be gone too.

Ernest Hemingway comes in from adventures, I walk him to his food, I have work to do.

He goes to his chair and I go to mine, trying not to

mind the mess, the waste, the fleeting,

and I write,

a word,

a line.

7. Seeking Wilderness

This morning I left,

didn't eat,

didn't dress,

on a mission for wilderness,

to be still and listen,

observe the wider kingdom.

I climbed the hillside, through silken cobwebs,

wild myself in wellies, hairpins, nightdress and intent.

Kept going till I reached the forest,

and was held back by a barbed wire fence.

I freed myself and stepped inside,

lay down in a sun filled tangle,

moss, holly, bramble.

Surrounded by tall trees,

sitka spruce and pine.

Their branches, like the plumes of burlesque

dancers,

fall and rise,

fall and rise.

8. Autumn

We were never less ready for autumn. The lovely golden time had lost its powers of seduction and no amount of swirling leaves or playful winds or fiery colouring could persuade us. For we were married to summer that year, and had put all our hopes and dreams of summers that had never come, into this long and perfect one.

We were never more together. We had savoured every heat filled second, lay on the baking ground, stared at the cloudless sky. Loving and mourning with every thought, with every breath and sigh.

But autumn came, slow, warm and gold.

Jane Gilheaney Barry

The fires stayed cold, the hedges stayed heavy with damsons and berries, and memories of summer yet. Nature was kind, let us linger awhile, in still bright evenings and warm sunshine. But soon her cooling breath stole the warmth from the sky, from our bones and the earth, and time went by.

Winter, hear me now. Do your worst, play your part. Send us your pain, your cold and dark. It matters not, time's pitiless march, for it's always summer in human hearts.

9. The Fall

The air changed first then came the feeling,

known to every living thing,

the change in season.

And from that moment,

no matter how the garden grew or hot the sun shone,

it was autumn.

No more the symphony of long grass, but of darkness,

No more the bright greens ceaseless bursting, but red and bronze and gold,

emerging from the boughs,

and gathering in the sweet earth beds,

where faded flowers bow their heads.

The light changed next,

and set the scene for fire ahead,

the year's last romance is the turning,

the most beautiful of them all,

before the dark end of the year, the fall.

10. *Winter is Coming*

The house and I, today we hide,

the fog has carried us away.

The outside world has vanished,

it wasn't real anyway.

To be sure, I walked over the cold green,

to the ghost trees,

right to the edge of darkness,

And reaching out my pale hand felt winter's grip in

the nothingness.

I'm ready to go in now.

11. November Morning

Fireside armchair.

She has one teddy and one purring friend.

Cosy pyjamas, little feet in.

Book, blanket, paper, pens.

12. Full of Yourself

Full of yourself, aren't you?

Yes.

I am full of myself,

I am whole,

without emptiness.

I wear no mask,

but don't try to define me.

I am not Irish, woman, mother, wife.

I have no shame, regrets, or envy.

I am free,

Richer than any man and any rule or god.

But tell me,

you, not full of yourself,

what are you full of?

13. I've Been

I've been editing my book,

and was much helped by an open window,

and the wind making the curtains billow.

I've been reclaiming the house after being away,

restoring energy,

clearing the pathways.

I've been walking out in the wind wild lane,

it is deeply alive and I feel the same.

I've been imagining a tree fall on me,

a reasonable fear,

two have already fallen this year.

14. *It's The Best Day Ever*

Sadhbh: People don't last forever do they?

Me: No, they don't

Sadhbh: Can I have a cracker now?

Me: Yes

Sadhbh: It's the best day ever, isn't it?

Me: As good as any day that ever was and ever will be.

15. *Spilling on to a Page*

I woke to rain.

Gusts of wind lifted the curtain,

to show slices of grey sky dripping.

I shivered, turned my pillow to the cold side, heaven.

Reached for glasses and my phone before remembering,

I'm on a phone and online break-ish for the weekend.

Though can someone please explain just how to do that,

when you've a daughter and a sister up in Dublin,

and parents,

and three other siblings?

Well you can't.

I keep it on the floor,

to protect my head from radiation,

but that's the best I can do.

Because let's face it, I can't protect my head from anything.

There's a small girl by the bed, she's enquiring if one of us will get up now.

And across the room an even smaller girl is sighing on Jimmy's couch.

She's been there since two a.m. or was it four?

'Hello Mammy, can I sleep on Jimmy's couch?' she asked.

'Yes, yes.'

Now I agree to get up,

but only long enough to do food, socks, dressing

gowns, tv, colours and coffee.

Then I'm back to bed with Daddy,

with the rain, notebooks and other books.

With plans and thoughts and possibility.

It's 6:40.

I'm a high functioning morning person, because of

the promise,

time.

Every day is the same, every morning I'm ecstatic,

and every day I'm sad come three o'clock.

The best days are those I start writing, drawing,

painting, even cleaning, instantly.

The reason this works is once I start, I can't stop.

When I can't stop, I'm happy.

If I don't spill on to a page I think,

and if I think too much, disaster.

I think I will get to editing/writing just as soon as···

and suddenly it's hours later.

But when I pour straight I'm invincible,

I can clear a swathe through everyday demands and
rain,

desires and domestic grind just, disappear.

I have a thing about paths.

I like to move,

unobstructed and fast.

'Girls, who blocked this path?

You know the paths must be clear.'

16. Writer Mammy Life

Blog down,

cat fed,

two children at school,

one in bed,

housework done,

fire lit,

looks like I might get a moment to sit.

Laptop open,

tea in hand,

word count flying,

feeling grand.

Moments like these, there aren't too many,

then it comes through the air, the familiar cry,

'MAMM…YYYY.'

2014

17. I Was Meant to be Editing

Don't think, that's the key.
When it comes to creative work,
control is your enemy.

Today we stayed in bed till 10 o'clock!
A sure sign we no longer have babies.
Don't get me wrong,
there were protests, but there was no one in need.
I will never have another baby,
this makes me happy indeed.

A terrible day weather wise, terrible and lovely.
Adrian put up some shelves.

Adrian put up the shelves,
and we painted the boxes.
I was meant to be editing,
I'm meant to be editing now,

but the box was calling,

and now it's these words.

Clearly, I need a dice.

Roll the dice,

tell me where to go.

Run my life.

No.

When it comes to painting I'm still afraid of canvas,

a box is less scary.

So breakfast, clean up, shelves going up, our girls

and I painting the boxes.

At first I was angsty.

My internal bitch editor was saying,

'What are you at?

You should be editing your book, not painting a box.'

She was right, of course,

only it doesn't matter.

Just when I was feeling lost I saw,

a horizon? A ship? And that was it.

I stopped thinking.

From this point I was in flow.

Then it was lunchtime, chats, clean up, groceries,

shelves up, jammies and Shrek on tv.

Where did the day go?

Now I'm having a glass of wine,

can you drink wine you've frozen?

I am.

It's raining still,

the fire is crackling,

the night is coming down fast.

Soon my friend will collect me and we will spill on to

a page,

without thought,

without edits,

and this day will end almost unnoticed,

almost.

Later in bed I will think,

tomorrow,

tomorrow I have such editing plans,

tomorrow,

we try again.

18. Turf

Now winter do your worst for the turf is home,

and the people sigh with pleasure.

For whatever happens we will all of us be warm,

come winter's storm.

19. Sisters & Pirates

Saoirse: Some of the ones at school said girls can't be pirates.

Me: Who said that?

Saoirse: It was only the boys.

Sadhbh: I'm fire girl! I wish I was a pirate.

20. With my restless soul, or as Shaylyn calls it, my OCD

With my restless soul or as Shaylyn calls it, my OCD,

I was feeling meh,

in need of inspiration, life, colour.

Adrian brought me Vogue.

I turned the pages, admired and yearned.

The heart grieves pleasure.

Escape without escaping,

of the home fires,

dark and winter,

the greyness of the every day,

domestic train.

Glamour, you see,

is still necessary to me.

But glamour in Leitrim's hard to come by,

Especially in winter.

Inspiration, life, colour.

I should have a party,

women only.

I will not go quietly into the country fog,

why can we not have glamour in a bog?

We can, we must. It is our duty,

as women and as living beings of beauty.

But you won't find it in Carrick at the weekend.

21. *April Fool's Day*

Today was sunny and warm and a good writing day and a good food day, and a good family day, plus funny.

I'd slept in. I woke up at seven aware of a weight on my feet, Sadhbh.

It's a new world of tired when you can sleep with a child on your feet.

As soon as I could I sat down for an hour to work on the book.

A few pancakes, hair bobbins, school bags, book work, and goodbyes later, it was just Sadhbh and me, and Shaylyn.

Sadhbh said, 'Mammy, can I look for rabbits please?'

'Where are you going to look for them?'

'In the sky.'

'Okay.'

'Yaaaay!'

Shaylyn is doing her Leaving Cert and stayed home to study, she has her Oral French today. I flitted about, tidying, thinking, we spoke French and talked college and future and music and hoped Sadhbh, worn out from her rabbit hunt, would go for a nap which she did in the end, at which point I got back to the book again.

I couldn't stop for a breath or for anything until coffee, though even with my eyes closing I resented the interruption, the time it took, the noise of making it, the chance of waking her up.

Coffee in hand and word count climbing and still I was fading and Sadhbh was now waking. I made more pancakes for the following morning. Then for lunch, I fried mushrooms in chilli with peppers, garlic and black olive pate. We ate this lovely saucy dish in the sunshine with cookbooks and pita bread and were getting back into our French when Sadhbh appeared covered in lipstick.

Her whole head. 'Nothing to problem about,' she said.

I was making dinner, because the cooking never ends, when Adrian and Saoirse came. She'd been in my mothers.

'I already had dinner,' she chirped.

'Okay,' I replied, 'I'll just give you a bit of the salad.'

'I had Brussels sprouts with it.'

'Wow.'

'So can I go out? Can I go on the swing, can I, can I?'

'Yes, you can go.'

Dinner and dishes, by bedtime it was still bright out and Saoirse announced she was hungry.

Turns out the 'dinner' in mums was an *April Fools* trick on us. I couldn't believe it!

'But what made you think to add Brussels sprouts to it?'

'I just thought it would sound good,' she said.

Stunned and impressed and hit suddenly at the breadth of life around me.

One Leaving Cert, one Junior Infant, one super Sadhbhy.

But *nothing to problem about*.

And tucking them into bed that night, I said to Sadhbh,

'Did you know, a little girl slept on my feet last night, I wonder who that was?'

And she said, 'I think it was Daddy.'

22. Corraleehan

My father came from the mountain, my mother from the valley.

Memories of my mother's home are older, from when we were younger, and full of sunshine.

The children of children born in the famine, these grandparents are harder to grasp. Patrick Fox is an old man in a sepia photograph.

He was the local storyteller, the man to whom people brought letters to read and forms to fill. He died before we were born but lives on in stories still.

My grandmother, Mary Susan Logan, was with us until I was six. She had long silver hair in a bun, gentle elegance. Her corner by the fire seemed dark at first but she'd draw you in, with emerald sweets and sweet smiling eyes.

Every time I see wild roses I think of her, the way they brushed her head that time we walked to the corner.

She loved music and dance and we'd dance for her, our shoes into slippers on her flagstone floor.

The lane from the road was long and it wound from high fields to a dip, a rugged place of fiery gorse, to golden crops and down again in verdant green to street and house.

Whitewashed walls of stone with pots of begonia and another plant I can't recall.

The blind goose who'd fought the fox and lived would make his way along the wall then turn triumphant at the gap. The black dog Jasper was always waiting for us at the end of the lane without fail. We didn't know our uncle Joe had told him we were coming, and set him on our trail.

Corraleehan was quiet in our childhood, a place for daydreams, but from our mother we knew it hadn't always been. And her stories of Corraleehan she painted so clear that I could see the young people coming over the hill at dawn from a dance as if they had just come that morning. Or the summer the house was re-thatched and they slept under the stars. I like to think of them.

Hay time in summer heat we'd hide under trees in the cool grass and one bonfire night we had a big fire there with our uncles Joe and Pat. It was one of those perfect evenings after a long hot day when the air is balm and the ground smells sweet. 'Listen,' my mother said.

'Listen to the sound of the corncrake, a bird of the past, we might never hear it again, this time might be the last.'

I tried really hard to imprint it in my head, only to find it was other things got printed there instead.

23. Joy Pockets

Me: Let's surprise Daddy and have the weeds and stones gathered before he gets home.
Sadhbh: Okay Mammy, he'll be so happy won't he?
Me: You're a bit hoarse, Sadhbh, have you a frog in your throat?
Sadhbh: No, but I've a rabbit in my pocket.

24. There's a Bird in the House

I spent my first nineteen years in a house looking out,

then two years of freedom,

two years and then back in a house.

Different houses, different places,

there I was,

wrapped in bricks, tiles, and mortar,

a wanderess,

a bolter,

a bird.

It was later I learned that the houses were places of

freedom,

they were always my gardens of Eden.

25. *Nature Cure*

I got up having not slept,

all night I tossed and rolled,

and I know what the problem is,

it's too much life to hold.

Morning filled my window,

'Jane, come out.'

I stepped into that morning new,

not sure of what I'd do or find,

I drive the weather or it drives mine.

It will be me I felt.

The sun a lie will not be warm,

the flowers will be all forlorn,

excepting for the tangle thorn when berries dark rot

sweetly.

The wind will rise before my eyes,

the trees will tremble at my sighs,

as I create the weather.

But I was wrong, was not to be,

it was the day created me.

The mellowest morn you've ever seen,

my eyes they went from dark to green.

Grateful to the wind that blew me,

that chilled me just enough to soothe me,

as I moved lightly through the scene.

'Alive it said, alive.'

I started back towards the house, the wind pulled

back my hair, 'Are you sure Jane? Going back there?'

'Oh yes, I have to tell about you, I can't go with you

yet.'

'We'll be here if you forget, forget us, or forget

yourself...'

26. It's Going Fast

It's night time in the garden.

I'm writing to the music of birds.

All around me the trees have turned shadowy black,

the grass is gone cold,

but the air is still sweet and there's heat in the walls

of the house at my back.

It's summer's last dance, our last chance to know it.

For we only get so many summers, don't blow it.

27. Nature Cure 2

The cat hates it when I move the furniture.

Sharing of darkness, we should all do that more.

So angry, I threw a big cooking spoon in the garden.

It was truly satisfying. Who knows why?

Or how the spoon came back, twice.

Major overwhelm,

malicious and ripe.

No, it is not hard, Jane.

The world is not free. But if we see we're alone and

are happy to be,

that is a kind of freedom.

And the smell of the turf fire alone is worth living for.

Every time I put newspaper down for painting the

same thing happens,

the death notices face up.

I have to study each one and then hide them.

I brought everything out in the garden,

urgency bubbling,

violence and paint,

spilling dread,

I could have saved time,

could have painted in the house instead,

without care for the surfaces.

But then I saw, a tiny creature in the paint.

I put the handle of my brush beside him, he clung on.

Held it gently to the wall and watched him step off,

We were both delighted.

The next one didn't fare as well, he was stuck fast to

the brush and paint.

I ran it gently through the long grass thinking,

he might fare better in that kingdom.

28. Rebel Versus the World

I love to move, to change, but I won't change for you.

I love to smile and see you smile but I won't smile for

you.

And I love charm but I'm not charming, and I can't lie

or bend or cry if that's what I'm expected to.

I love the extra mile, I own that mile, but not for you,

and not your rules.

I love to win but I won't do the things you say I need

to do to win, and couldn't if I wanted to.

I love to hide but I can't hide when it's the time to

speak, or stand for something in my heart feels right.

And I love peace but can't pretend it's mine or things

are fine or say, they should be left alone.

I won't,

don't ask,

because I can't.

29. Sadhbh's Letter to Santy

Dear Santy,

Sadhbh Barry has been a good girl⋯ to Saoirse,
ehm⋯tries not to cry or be naughty.

She would love a clock,

a moon that can tell the weather,

a star, a necklace, a yoyo, a cowgirl hat, an elf, a
princess, a book and a box, a treasure box, a pirate
hat and dress, a telescope and eye patch, a bouncy
boat and a singing teapot.

Love Sadhbh

30. 'As summer storms were her favourite,
as rough winds raised the curtain.'

2015

31. What to do about January?

It's 4:40 pm so I'm struggling.

It's the dark you see,

when it closes in it closes me.

I love all weather, all seasons, but the dark and I
don't agree.

I like to breathe and I can't breathe in the dark,

country dark,

specifically,

is darker.

32. Dear Dublin

Dear Dublin,

It was wonderful, for I am bored here now. There is
no colour, no nourishment. And it's not the few
people I love who are all worth staying afloat for.

And it's not my house that I've conjured, can paint all
the shades that are in me,

Jane Gilheaney Barry

but the cold hard winter never ending, like a grey sea.

I survive, always,
though my internal world still demands filling.
Writing, learning, reading,
all the good stuff.
Survival isn't enough.

Like a garden where even the richest darkest soil will
lose its richness if the crops are not rotated often, I
have lost something, I feel will return with the spring.
Here this time of year, you can't depend on anything.
On walks, or the children at school, or as a new driver
on driving,
not even those minor freedoms.

So here I am, rooted in darkness, craving light,
culture, adventure, and I would go anywhere.
But then when the chance comes I am anxious, find it
hard to go.
That is how rooted I am and how far,
like so many women,

trying to bloom where we are.

And in the days before I left I almost sabotaged myself.

It all seemed so difficult. Why is it so difficult? To untangle oneself?

The children are no longer babies and though it's been some years I have taken this train a thousand, no, ten thousand times. At the point of tears I think how the universe is conspiring to stop me, then I laugh, I know it is only me.

I was going now to see my eldest daughter in a fashion show. To buy some new clothes, to fill the well, restore some sanity. The day I left was of course, mad.

Endless instructions and cleaning, and leaving things just so, you know, in case I get hit by a bus, never get to come back. And groceries, in case they all starve.

Sadhbh tells me how much she will miss me and cups my chin.

I tell everyone how much I love them. I feel guilty. You might think I'm crazy and though I agree, you only think that if you're not like me. Caught, in the domestic web.

Leaving home I can hardly breathe, but on the train I read. Once in Dublin I'm breathing again, the air is good. It is already warmer than Leitrim though the next few days will be biting cold, I feel better.

My sister Martha meets me, full of the joys of that spring I crave. We make our way through the old familiar streets without having to think, and I ponder how I used to meet her off the train as a child, and now we are going to see my child. And though time flies I am not sad or even nostalgic because it feels right. I know I am more confident now, even if trips make me guilty, give me stage fright.

At the venue we've time, buy a bottle of wine, and share the most wonderful talk. The kind that runs on in perfect sparking harmony, like a dance. We come together quickly in thought, then still in synch move apart, before coming together again, it is perfect but short.

Seeing Shaylyn on the runway's a thrill. I'm her mother so when she appears the world turns invisible. She is striking, my girl. Has started to inhabit herself. I always feel sorry for teens, the way they are not yet at home in their skin. But she will be twenty this year, and has a calm presence that's good to be near.

It's Monday as I write this, we woke under a blanket of snow that's falling heavy again now, beautiful. I hate it so.

The fire's crackling and the house is quiet, I have to go…

33. Alive

Sadhbh – Is everything alive, Saoirse?

Saoirse – I think not everything.

Sadhbh – But how can we know the alive things?

Saoirse – Because they're always changing. Like the trees.

Sadhbh (shocked) – The trees are alive?!?!

34. *Writing, Inching Forward*

Hello from my kitchen to wherever you are.

I had such a good day of editing yesterday, I felt limitless after it. I thought, I have to keep this going, but it's been a struggle this morning.

Even with my smallest girl taking a nap, it just seemed impossibly hard, as it does sometimes, as it is.

I knew if I didn't inch forward, if I wasted the nap, I'd be furious with myself, so I did what I had to do, I forced it.

I put my phone away, sat down in the kitchen and I made myself read the next line, read it ten times, twenty times, change this, change that, move this part, change that part. Like wading through tar I'd describe it.

In the end I just stayed for as long as I had. Time is a luxury. Most days I get pulled away fairly consistently, or at the turning point of when it's going well. The worst is being pulled away when I know I can do more still. And every day I have to start again. Today ended up not a bad day, not the best, but certainly not the worst. I'll be back at it again in the morning bright and early.

Inching forward⋯

35. The dream is for the house to disappear, more overgrown with every passing year. And me with it.

36. Still Editing

As you know, I'm editing my first novel. This is my fourth draft⋯or fifth draft? I've lost count, all I know is this is the most detailed, painstaking one yet. It's difficult to say exactly how long I can spend on just one paragraph or one sentence but;

hours,

hours,

hours.

I want in, I get in, I have to leave, I need to get back again.

Years.

37. I seek advice on managing time for my writing...

The world said it had no answer. Especially not for mothers.

Mum said she felt not many would have done it with small children, they would have waited.

Jane Gilheaney Barry

My artist friend Madeleine said;

'*It's difficult to manage your time with small children but if you wait until they are older there's the very real danger of never getting started at all.*'

Dad said I should start the next book.

Lol.

38. Nature Cure 3 (April)

I woke in a sunbeam, the red squirrel is back, I watched him run up the ash tree.

'Did you hear the foxes?' you asked.

'Yes.'

'And did you see the stars?'

'Yes, they were not very far.'

'And did you hear the birds?'

'Yes.'

'So you had a good night?'

'It feels like a brand new life.'

39. And I'm tired of being tired, and miserable and flattened by things. Aren't you?

40. Mondays

Mondays don't bother me anymore because I'm at home, and the things that drive me crazy happen every day.

Routine, schedules, mess, writing, not writing, laundry, and the dishwasher.

If anything, I love Mondays, in the same way I love all beginnings, mornings, even January.

Fresh starts,

possibility…

41. Nature Cure 4

Sunday morning I went round the house, like a tempest,

cleaning, de-cluttering,

a woman possessed.

All the usual frustration, over all the work I want to do and can't.

After that,

we went to the mountain.

The rain was so heavy,

the mist so thick,

we could barely see more than a few feet of road,

tree tops and slivers of ditch.

I rolled the window down so I could feel more a part of it.

I said to Adrian, 'See how it moves, I wish it would pick me up, move me, carry me away over the tree tops. Wouldn't you like that to happen to you?'

'Oh yes,' he replied, for he's used to me.

And he comes from the mountain too.

Sometimes I'm more than my body can handle.

And sometimes I just feel so limited.

That's when I crave the elements, and want their freedom for myself.

Sunday evening in the house.

Shaylyn gone back to college, seafood dinner, journal, red wine. As night fell the family watched tv, I watched the fire, shadows on a blank page lengthening, listening, to the falling rain.

Monday, begin again···

42. There are times in life when writing is a greater ally than love, or anything else in this world.

43. *The Layers That Envelop Me* (September)

It is strange and good to be alone, the family's at work and school. There isn't a sound here, not even a cat. I already walked him to his food, he likes me to do that.

Now he's out there somewhere, in the mist and long grass.

I've been out there too, taking air, taking photographs, under a sky that's almost blue.

I close the gates,

that freedom feeling.

I come inside and see,

Sky, mist, gates, house,

windows full of trees.

And at the centre,

writing,

me.

44. To Be Free (December)

A survivor,

fae,

wild creature,

figment of imagination, mine.

It's been a fight from birth,

to live free for my time on this earth.

A mystery they say,

blood of the aliens.

I can't be helped, but can help sometimes,

with my blood like wine.

A wanderess putting roots down,

head in clouds,

still journeying.

Elemental,

I am the wind wild gentle,

always moving,

carry you with me.

Woman, rebel, force of nature.

Tearing old worlds down.

It's never too late to choose your fate,

be swept away,

on a different current,

to move, to burn.

When the day comes and you waken,

know you never can return.

2016

45. So I'm an INTP (January)

The family concurred, with much conspiratorial laughter,

that the results were me. And the only proof anyone needed, that the test works perfectly.

In short...

'I'm interested in... intellectual stimulation, more than anything else. And have no time for or interest in daily life including self care or maintenance.'

'Eccentric, creative, analyser. And don't talk to me about celebrities.'

That can't be true.

46. Today While Editing

I veered between exhaustion, almost falling asleep at the laptop,

to getting so absorbed in one scene that when the cat moved, I screamed the roof off, to feeling daunted at all the work still to do,

to not feeling up to it at all,

to feeling determined, bloody minded,

to feeling hungry, thirsty, wanting to eat something nice, but deciding on something handy instead to save time.

Keeping the fire alive,

letting the cat in, out, in again,

thinking about Game of Thrones,

thinking about the children, thinking about you,

giving a bee a drink from a spoon,

thinking about all the other things I want/need/would love to do instead of this.

REMINDING myself that THIS, no matter how hard or impossible, IS my number one priority, and all I really need to work on now.

And I did get some work done,

somehow···

47. Writing Magic (June)

I've been carried away in a beautiful sea,

of thoughts and words rushing through me.

I try to capture the pearls, but before I can, they turn

into sea foam and are gone.

I worried, there were so many.

Had I nets enough to hold and carry?

But perhaps I didn't need to?

Perhaps the sea was enough, it would hold them all

forever, hold me too, and nothing would be ever lost.

Even as I had that thought I was swept in another

direction.

It was glorious,

and never ending.

48. I want to live intensely.

Intensely or not at all.

49. A Day in the Life (June)

Coffee and blog post to finish and share,

lunches and breakfast,

finding things,

hair.

Social media,

clear up,

nothing to wear.

No interruptions for writing today, as the youngest at

playschool, then a friend's house, hurrah.

Writing and housework,

no time for siestas,

water plants,

do the laundry,

make a Pasta Puttanesca.

Painted,

kept it simple,

water colours,

cheapo ones.

Bedtime for small girls.

Cuddles, teeth, chats,

searching for this and that,

protracted negotiations,

collapse.

Watched the sun go down,

wrote in my journal,

had a gin and tonic,

pottered around.

Shaylyn and Adrian are not home yet.

I'm writing and the house is quiet, except for the
dark.

Going down to make tea.

Will carry a notebook, a book, and two pens with me.

Will feel restless, dream of morning, yet resist going
to bed.

Will write again, a list or ten,

chat with Shaylyn and Adrian when they get in,

check my phone now and then.

Wait for tomorrow, begin again…

50. Advice From Sadhbh, 5.

'When it's not working out close your eyes.'
(June)

51. *Note to Self* (June)

Just read a chapter, that's all you have to do. And if something jars, if it doesn't flow right, change it. That's all. Nothing big, nothing difficult. Just read it.

52. *Reasons to Be Cheerful.* (July)

I'm at my desk in the laundry room,

with books, notebooks and plants.

My favourite coffee mug is by my side,

the one I bought on Thomas St in 1995.

It's a wet grey morning, very still.

The window's open to the hill.

The air has a name.

It's scent of sky, and earth, and rain.

So pure, it's like no one ever used it before.

53. *I Always Write Well in September···* (August)

Late August and nights closing in,

the air's different,

the freshness of summer is gone.

While I'll miss it and long for its light, there are embers still.

Soon autumn will burst into flame,

earth and air cool again,

I'll look forward, remember,

I always write well in September.

54. *Like a Phoenix*

In false arenas I was dreaming while my spirit yearned for meaning, like a phoenix I set fire to myself.

Comfort, safety held no healing, in my soul already leaving, knowing worse would be a phrenic living death.

Embraced the edict for the zenith, my existence craved the burning, wrote the lyrics, found and hunted, let it all go up, in flames.

From my ashes, fire tested, like a phoenix I arose again.

Now more powerful than ever, like the sun I rise forever, fan the flames of other fires once begun.

And like Venus, stars surround me, see my spirit, feel my power,

know I won.

55. Summer Never Arrived (September)

We were promised one day of summer,

but clearly something went wrong.

I woke early in an autumn mist.

I had hoped to see the sun rise,

but the sky had hidden it.

My eye fell as it always does, on the forest.

I went there once before, with Dad, in the real
summer.

To immerse ourselves, explore.

We loved it, though it tried to kill us.

It is a fortress,

almost impenetrable.

Inside you can barely stand,

and where you can the plant life comes up to your
head,

and where you can't, it closes in and presses down on you instead.

It is a place teeming, overflowing with life, a true wildness.
Before we went I had wanted to go.
I was at a low ebb, and one tree to another, I thought it might help.
Now I dream about it, and I don't mind, that it never dreams of me.

Today it lay in its veils of mist, pretending innocence and silence.
I struck out with a peaceful joy to go to it.
I walked over the still green lane, where a hare had just passed under the chestnut trees, and climbed over a rusted fence.
With rush clumps for stepping stones, I navigated the edges.

In the grey sea sky and half dark, I was soon soaked
to my senses.

Next I was blown away, through a sea of diamond
cobwebs,
Where light rose rich from fallen leaves,
lost summer tears.
Discovering you, dark seasons,
stealing years.

56. I am a Winter House

The house is new, built a few years ago, but the way
it writes poems you'd never know.
The house is a ship, it carries dreams, today it
captured Halloween.
I blinked and the trees on the hill turned russet, I only
opened the door for a moment.
In rushed the thin air, dark for the corners, scent of
rain and turf smoke,
and the house wrote,
I am a winter house...

2017

57. Who would join me here in the firelight,

with rain and smoke, on the edge of night.

With wine to drink and tales to spill, and

fairy folk drifting over the hill⋯ (January)

58. I am stronger than you.

59. *In terms of mood I've been* (April)

In the kitchen sunlight flowed in, and I made the most beautiful dinner. Trout fillets, seasoned and fried in butter and a little oil. Keeping them warm I added more butter to the pan with slivers of almonds, handfuls of spinach to wilt and anointed with lemon.

Heaven,

literally heaven.

It's been cold for so long, I've taken to wearing a big old dressing gown.

I get up, I get dressed, I put on my make-up. I tie my hair up in a knot.

And then I throw the big dressing on top.

It's glamour deconstructed for the chilly, not so chilled, lady writer.

I said to Martha (my sister), 'I have to have my hair up for doing anything.'

And she said, 'It depends, up for writing, but down for say, killing a man.'

And If I'm writing I throw a blanket over my legs and wrap it around my feet.

Folks, I couldn't get up if I tried, I am literally frozen to the seat.

But this cold spell, I walk around the garden most nights, thrilled to the changes, some returning flower or other. It is April still, but May is coming, and the garden knows.

Every year I wait for the lilac to bloom; we have two, one purple, one white. Then I'm sad at the short time it has.

But it was after eight before the sun went down tonight.

I stood facing the west, let it pour into me.

With the light, the surround sound, the orchestra of birds, from three clusters of forest, I did feel as if I'd had some kind of cosmic cleansing experience.

So ended the spell of April in me, from storm to calm, from cold to warm, of scents, and tastes, and longing, letting go.

I am myself again, I know.

...

April 28th state of atmosphere? Much improved.

60. Inspiration is the drug, creativity and change are the way

61. I am a Summer House

The house is new, built a few years ago, but the way it writes poems you'd never know. The house is a ship, it carries dreams, today it captured shimmering things.

I blinked and the hill turned lush with flowers. I'd only opened the door for an hour.

In rushed the green air,

light for the corners,

scent of lilacs and clover,

and the house wrote,

I am a summer house···

62. Seasons Turn (May)

Another luminous day. The countryside is overflowing. Cascades of flowering hawthorn, the swallows returned, and the lilacs.

All filling the air with ecstasy.

The last of the trees leafed suddenly, like waves rolling, glimmering, turning the light green.

The alliums came back yesterday, the laburnum on Tuesday. I was afraid my delphiniums weren't going to make it, but I can see their bright leaves and stalks just beginning, shooting out of the earth, starting their long journey up to meet hollyhock, gladioli, and lupin.

They get a much longer time, those later flowers, to linger,

turn to seed and sculpture.

But the flowers of May come and go so fast.

It's like a dream, a bright beautiful dream that doesn't last.

63. Limitless (October)

I woke to a morning of gold and rustling trees, with a surprising blue sky and bright sunlight. The birds are delighted and sing as brightly as if it were summer. The garden is unmoved. It lies cool, flowers fading, under a mantle of dew.

But out in the field there's a blaze of montbretia. Every morning I stop to admire its bright dance through the muted colours, the browns and greens. I think it must have escaped from some garden or other. It is *mad* alive. Strong, giddy with freedom. I understand. On blustery days or in times of escape I feel more alive too, the blood rises. Autumn is stirring to wild things, and every season is good for the people. The changes they bring.

This morning after everyone left I stood a while on the step with my face turned to the sun.

I will just as likely do that when the rain comes.

64. *The Power* (October)

Writing has brought me on an unexpected journey.

It sparked awakening,

plunged me into depths I never knew before,

showed me all the light and darkness in me,

saved me,

returned me to my core.

When the knocks came in the dead of night,

I opened the door.

There have been many intensifications,

now there's more of me than was before.

The lights are on. The witch is home, and it's glorious.

It's like that Secret Garden quote, 'Is the spring coming?' he said. 'What is it like?'··· 'It is the sun shining on the rain and the rain falling on the sunshine···'

It is the meeting, the coming together of many things.

Of coming through things,

Of deep writing that is deep meditation,

that works on the inner landscape,

It is previously repressed spirit, newly released.

It's when you know the world is hurt and you'd like to

help, and even, just to be happy is revolution in itself.

It's detachment and connection.

It is the seasons too,

autumn now,

leaves falling now.

Hour by hour.

By the power of creativity, nature, and intent, we

have the power.

65. I create things which don't exist because I want them to

66. *Mothering* (October)

The sun came out by mid-morning, gentle, golden.

When it comes to a little patient the face never lies.

She hates the white calpol. In vain we protest, 'But it's made with strawberries!'

'They must have been green,' she replies.

By afternoon it's raining. I have my sick child and my nephew, my new blog baby, Cuan. He's nine months and cute as a button. It's not easy being nine months either but how much easier to care for a child that age!

I'd forgotten.

It's exhausting certainly, but with effort and intent you can be absolutely brilliant at it. With older children it's the emotional work that's important.

Like all mothers I am terrified of dying. I don't think they've ever needed me as much as they do now, until they do again. I want to always be there. And at the other end there's Shaylyn, turning twenty-two.

Graduating soon, working and thriving in Dublin. It gives me the greatest happiness to think of her. You still worry, of course, but it's different.

By ten the house is quiet again,

the night is black and wild with wind.

67. If You Throw Stones at Her, She'll Use Them to Build Something (November)

It's a writing day and a day for the fire. Grey out and bitterly cold, with flashes of brilliant sunlight. I've never been so strong or happy.

Life is funny. We're up, and then we go down again,

like a wave,

or a flower.

But we can use the downs as much as the ups for deeper creative work and growing. There's a saying, don't throw stones at her, she'll use them to build something.

The creative path is one with few guarantees, except you.

Strong, fulfilled, resilient you. And in return, with every word, hundreds of thousands of words, I have grown. In every direction, deeper, higher, out of reach, and out of this world.

68. Writing Seasons

Today I'm with the creativity book, a project I started last year. Do you remember? I wrote the first draft in a few weeks. It just flowed, and I thought I'd have it published in no time. After all, it was only 5000 words.

Well that didn't happen.

Because it kept on flowing.

To spring, and 40,000 words.

To summer, with illustration.

Much like the novel I felt that to follow was the best course of action.

All spring and summer it flowered, then with autumn it deepened, grew richer.

Now that it's winter it will follow the trees again, and be pared back to structure.

Jane Gilheaney Barry

69. *My New Dress Has Pockets* (November)

I've worn different selves, like different dresses, worn
for a while then discarded.
Some I've forgotten, some left behind, some worn
often. According to need or environs.
But at some point, we have to get back,
to our one true self.
I can see now I was lucky. I learned very early,
through various summers and storms,
how to stand alone.
I will not return.
I'll send words, messages,
like stones rippling still waters.
Piercing the surface, lodging themselves in the deep.
My new dress has pockets,
and fits like a dream.

70. A Perfume in the Air, A Sigh on the Pavement (November)

A beautiful day in Dublin. The Celtic new year, the first day of winter, and my daughter's college graduation. How did it feel?

It was like a dream, surreal. I don't think I ever imagined the future, now for a moment it's here.

I've always loved the sense of history in our capital city. You don't have to know it, just walk the streets. It's in the stones, layer on layer, of other times and other players.

The city, the air, the light is the same. There is history, yes, and indifference. It is we have moved on; it is we have seen changes.

Today she moved over the stage as her name was called. The same way she moves through the city now.

I've always been good with transitions. She was the
loveliest of children, but I have delighted in watching
her go, and will yet.
And I didn't cry until I wrote these words, and I don't
know why I cry now.

I savoured it all.
Perhaps that's how I know,
where the light falls,
on the warm brick, the cold stone,
and beloved faces.

How the tree leafs,
and the bough breaks,
and we keep on,
keep moving on.
Leave our own imprint.
A perfume in the air,
a sigh on the pavement.

2018

71. *Country Life* (January)

Went over the lane tonight in the pitch dark, pyjamas
and wellies.

To share wine with Colm, my brother.

And found my way home again after.

72. *In the Bleak Mid-Winter*

Comfort is a kitchen table,

a powerful place.

There is no territory beyond the table, we know that
now.

We've been living life in darkness without edges.

Only endless, infinite space surrounds us.

Outside has faded in mist,

even the walls of the house disappeared.

Only the tables are lighted,

floating islands of cheer.

73. No 73

Come,

sit here,

dream,

create something.

74. Found Poem...

Ah but she was beautiful.

Come, trace back,

see her beauty and remember,

how it was then,

better.

75. Feeling Energy (February)

I love the Sitka Spruce.

I love how the sun filters through, and the songs they

sing, especially in high wind, like music.

I can't help thinking of summer, and when I think

about summer I feel twenty-one.

I would much rather feel twenty-one than be twenty-one.

I kept the music playing, all day long,

it wafted through the house,

in the most mysterious way.

So that I could feel it everywhere,

the new energy.

76. *The Call of the Wild* (February)

What were we seeking?

Signs of spring,

Wildness,

Promise of summer.

The indefinable thing, that we go to the mountain for.

Even though I can't define it, I know it in others.

And I know it in me.

77. *What You Are*

This is the world of men,

the one we've built.

But step off the tar,

you enter another world,

you remember what you are.

78. *Dauntless* (March)

How hard am I willing to work for it?

Harder than anyone else.

I want to write the best book I can,

publish it.

Do it again.

My idea of success?

Push myself,

be myself,

as far as I can.

I want to be able to say,

I did everything I could,

I used everything I was given,

I excavated and alchemised everything,

love and pain.

I railed against what you'd call limits.

And I'd do it again.

79. We Returned From the Mountain

*We returned from the mountain renewed,
restored.
Covered in dirt but cleansed to the core.
Happy as if something great had occurred.*

80. Witch Life (April)

Blaze of whin,

harbouring witches.

Burn my domain,

if you dare.

I will transform into a hare.

Coursing streams,

leaping ditches,

flame again.

81. Bloom Time (April)

Woke to the most perfect morning. Birds singing, warm sun at last.

Tomorrow is the 1st of May. Even if I didn't know this I could mark it by the air and by the lilacs.

Every year I watch for their arrival and then mourn their passing that comes too soon. I find it amazing but no matter how the sun shines they won't stay any longer. It's beautiful and sad at once, we only have them for a month.

Also blooming now, and briefly, are our tulips, all red. White and pink flowering cherries, two magnolias, and six native flowering trees, all white. I don't recall the name.

They line the driveway to our door.

I wish I had a million more.

A sea, a forest.

They give the house a light, romantic air.

We have all this space, and not the time, nor means to fill it. But leave it to nature. Dandelions, buttercups, and daisies, blooming everywhere.

The fields are turning green.

If you listen you can hear the earth's heart beating, the air is fresher than it's ever been.

Meanwhile, it's lambing season still. Our raised beds project, we call it the *medicine wheel*, is coming on. For the next few weeks I'll be working on the novel. My last chance to work on it alone. From June I'll be working with an editor,

ahead of publication in September.

82. Mood (April)

I've a short window of time and there's a cat crying under it.

So I'm thinking. About all the things.

No sleep last night, the books I want to write, my (stalled) work in progress, how messy the house is, 'Home of the Year' on tv tonight, dinner - what we're having.

I'm thinking about Dad,

about Mum,

about evil Parkinson's,

about Adrian, and how lambing is going, and how I miss him, this time of year.

I'm thinking about the girls, about swimming lessons, school woes, and driving lessons I still have to do. About letting the dog in, and the cat out, and the other cat in, and feed them.

Feed the plants too.

Answer the emails.

About the laundry that needs to be hung or be washed again,

the deadline I missed for the novel competition,

how cold it is, and grey, my hair, the day.

I put on another dressing gown. I pour myself a gin.

On the stairs there's an apple core, we all walked past it for days.

Today I picked it up.

Motherhood.

Chicken for dinner, and spuds, and new cabbage, sautéed in butter.

With toasted fucking almonds, out of pure defiance.

Is it Easter yet? Because I can't wait, for the routine break.

Footprints in the hall,

great grey dirty ones, and small muddy ones, and animal ones,

plus a moth,

three flies,

and a bee.

I knocked him into a hat with a makeup brush and set him free.

Outside it's raining, birds singing, wind winding.

No wait, sun is shining, and the blackthorn is blooming, in all the dark places,

while the cherry is too light, too pure.

That's the trouble with April. Where nothing is settled. Especially me.

83. *Eat well, dress well, and tell stories.* (May)

One thing that was as true about me at four as it is at forty-four is that I always wanted to eat well, dress well, and tell stories.

What I only realised in recent times is that eating well and dressing well are also stories. Outward expressions of inner things, identity, richness and longings. It's best when they all come together but to pull any one off is fulfilling.

Like last night's dinner. It could not have been simpler.

I had some beautifully fresh hake fillets and I made a light batter of flour, eggs, pepper, sea salt, and cold water. I cut the fish into strips, dipped in the batter, and fried until golden in a deep pan of blistering hot olive   oil.

We ate it in the garden with wedges of lemon, and on the side, potato salad with herbs from the garden, mint, parsley, sage, basil, and oregano, washed down with an ice cold prosecco.

The whole seawater, citrus, sea freshness vibe, just right for a hot summer evening.

84. *Two nights in the garden in May I've spent*

Two nights in the garden in May I've spent. From haze of sunset, until a full bright moon appeared over the tree tops.

I thought the birds would break their hearts with singing.

The garden is an amphitheatre.

It is the venue, the audience, and the performer.

The play is joyous and gentle.

I am surrounded in beauty,

earthly, profound, celestial.

85. How To Become An Extreme Writer···

Write every day until it becomes a habit.

Ignore 'the voices.'

Write in any conditions, anytime, anywhere.

Write rough, write poorly, but write.

Write when you don't feel like it.

Write until you can't imagine a life without writing.

Choose writing over other things you enjoy/want to do.

Write until you've found healing, awe, flow, ecstasy, joy.

Write until you have to.

Write until it's hard to know where writing ends and you begin.

Declare yourself a writer.

Be writing.

86. The Wild Already Knows

Believe in your creative power.

You already know what you want to do so put it out there in thoughts, in actions, and in words.

Who will disagree with you?

Not the wild.

Like you, the wild already knows...

87. Dark Pursued Her

Dark pursued her··· snap of twigs, silken, silver mist, igniting, vivid, rolling in, moon rising, clear and brilliant.

88. All or Nothing (May)

In the end it's all about magic.

We want magic.

We want enchantment.

We're wired for it.

In the blood.

89. When Shaylyn asked 'What are you writing?' (June)

Like the will of the wind,

cold inside,

What made you a witch?

Have you ever left yourself?

Trying to identify what it was,

that made her snap?

That marginal place,

some call home,

Where clocks have no power,

Where spirit people are free to roam,

Ruled by imagination,

enchanted by stones, sensorially explosive,

I am stronger than you know.

Always seeking,

Why a highly sensitive being needs so much

sensation, I don't know.

But I never missed anything.

I never miss.

I was born a writer,

I was born a witch.

90. *Writing Daze* (July)

Another beautiful and exhausting day with heat and the book. I can't decide if I'd rather be done now or take a break then have another go at it. I just came out to catch the last of the evening sun and to pick two heads of broccoli. I'm in a writing daze and hungry but not sure what would satisfy me. There's no food in the house that won't take too long to cook so roast broccoli it is, with ginger, soy sauce, and chilli. And the house is a mess, the worst it's ever been. It never ceases to amaze me how quick it falls apart, if I don't keep working at it.

91. September – I Published My First Novel 'Cailleach~Witch.'

And the girls aged six, nine, and twenty-two said, 'Mammy, we're so proud of you.'

92. At peace and yet somehow on fire...

About the Author

Jane Gilheaney Barry is an author and founder of *That Curious Love of Green*, a creative lifestyle brand that embodies her philosophy of creativity as a way of life.

She lives outside Ballinamore, Co. Leitrim, in the north west of Ireland, with her husband Adrian and children, Saoirse and Sadhbh. Her eldest daughter, stylist Shaylyn Gilheaney, lives in Dublin.

Jane is the author of the successful, genre defying novel *Cailleach~Witch*. She is currently working on two prequels, *Banshee* and *Changeling*, the story of Ellen Cleary. She's also working on two more books in this series, That Curious Love of Green cookbook and a title on creativity.

Cailleach~Witch

What readers are saying about Cailleach~Witch

'This is genre-bending stuff, that weaves together fantasy, fairy-tale and Gothic to deliver a fast-paced, atmospheric thriller. As with many Irish writers (e.g. John McGahern, who incidentally comes from the same county as Jane) the sense of place and tradition is very strong. The atmosphere is broody and foreboding, while the plot moves quickly, forward and backwards through time, with many unexpected twists and turns. I was reminded more than once of Daphne du Maurier, especially Jamaica Inn: Cailleach too creates a beautiful and desolate setting for love, tragedy and maybe a new beginning. I thoroughly enjoyed this stylish novel.'

'This is the most energy transcending witch novel I have read. I felt like I was truly in Ireland, I could feel the energy of the story as if I was there, as if I could manifest the story into life.

Jane has a way with the rhythm of her stories. She is able to push the energy right to you.'

'I just had to reread each vivid description of the wilderness and the elements that surround the mysterious house wherein the Cleary family of women live for the setting itself is a character in the book. Barry knows the stuff of which a good story is made.'

'This book is a spell - a spell cast with a deep understanding of humanity, its relationship to nature and to women who embody the power of difference. It is not a singular story, it is a multiple of lives woven together to compose a larger story

130

and the author has done this weaving with great dexterity. Cailleach no doubt deserves a larger audience and I would love to see it turned to a series one day - it carries that sort of potential, being suited to the times we live in. This is a story we needed, and now it exists.'

'Other worldly, and almost dystopian. You feel disappointed that you the reader must by definition be one of the weak 'human' townspeople because you would so like to be one of these noble tribe of gifted women.

'The imagery in this book is second to none, from the moment you dip your head in you will be surrounded by the atmosphere, the house, the women, the mountain, the village and the suspense. If I was to compare it to anything I think it would be a cross between Practical Magic and Sinead DeValeras Irish Fairy Tales.'

Read on for the first chapter of Cailleach~Witch

Chapter 1

The Waiting

Erin

Summer was passing us by, growing heavy. I was in the garden with Honor and too many butterflies, too much gravity, and a cool glass of wine, when the black dog came shuffling up the lane with the sky on his back.

'The girls are returning,' Honor said.

I followed her gaze to the mountain. This time we were ready. She went back to her deadheading, me to my wine, but everything was different now.

The family comings and goings are marked always with one form or other of storm. On the day the girls came, dark clouds rumbled low in a sky turbulent since dawn. *Dark things to come*, I thought with interest as I gathered some interest myself among the throngs at Dublin airport. I'd been standing, hands on hips, my face turned to the maelstrom above.

Ten years before, we sent them away – after the incident, when the people turned on them. This kind of thing happened sometimes. It wasn't the girls' fault. They couldn't help what they were, and the townspeople couldn't help but take their chance for rage when it came along. A combination of fear and need is a difficult one.

It wouldn't have lasted, of course. They'd never drive us out, not that we could go. We were tied to that place as the mountain itself and with the wisdom of ages we knew – when modern medicine failed them and they couldn't find comfort or cure, it was back to us they would come, eager for the charms, the healing herbs, the water, and the hands.

Ours was a last chance for many, and no one would forget it soon, but Aunt Mae had been right. There was no need for the young girls to suffer it. Their time here would come soon enough and the mountain would have its way, but not yet. We sent for their father.

As light broke on the appointed day, grey morning mist morphed into swirling clouds, as if stirred by an angry invisible hand, and the wind cried with bone chilling eeriness. We worked calm and fast to batten the hatches, greenhouse, garden, animals, house, nothing new. Marius was our concern, driving in these conditions and still hours away. We were close, much more, you might call it, attuned to the elements than regular folk. We'd invoked protection from the Cailleach's wrath, but there was still a chance he wouldn't make it.

All we could do now was wait, and we stood, the old aunts Ellen and Mae, my twin Honor, our nieces and me. My chest tightened with pain for the waiting, the silence, and what we must do. The clocks struck one.

'It's time,' said Mae.

We made our way through the rooms, a quiet determined procession, while all around us the house creaked and swayed as an old ship forlorn for the parting. Living here, I often imagined, was like living at sea, though none of us had ever seen it. I thought too of the difference; a ship is free.

In the hall the volume of elements rose, and the temperature dropped along with my resolve. What if he wasn't there, hadn't made it? And what if he was? Were we doing the right thing? But without so much as a glance for us or each other, Mae and Ellen, like gladiators meeting the crowd, heaved and threw open the door. In rushed the darkness, the stinging rain, the monstrous wind. I was aware just for a moment of so much hair, jet, gold, slate and vermillion, filling the air then falling in waves of slow motion. But there was no time to lose in dreaming. Honor led Drew and I led Devin out and down the treacherous steps to the lane and their father there, waiting.

We turned for Dara, tight lipped and pale as a changeling but steady and coming alone. Looking up to the house, the mountain above, the sky on top, it felt as if any minute the whole lot might come crashing down. No words were spoken, the handover swift, brutal. What could any of us say? We stepped back to the wall, back up the stone steps, like sentries who know the drill well and are weary of it. When we got to the top we stopped, turned, and watched them.

'There go the roses,' said Ellen.

As the car pulled away Devin and Drew looked back. It had comforted them, to see our calm exteriors illuminated in the doorway, and they watched for as long as the forest would let them. We didn't move or bow our heads. We were used to the storm, to that life in the shadow of the mountain. I supposed that Dara heard the sound as we did, that she steeled herself against it much as we were doing. She was strong for her age and not once did she turn around. I admired her grit. Someday she was going to need it, we all would.

We watched the car as it slowly snaked the road, sometimes visible, sometimes only the lights through the forest. Once we knew not only that they'd made it down but that they'd crossed the bridge at town, we invoked the elements into a banishing.

For how long, we wondered? Not forever, we knew, but our hearts were still broken. It was a strange thing to send and to wish them away when we needed them with us so badly.

'Safe away little birds,' said Mae.

The air was still now.

After that was a hard time for us, and for Honor especially, but life soon went on as before. We were strong enough, the two sets of two sisters, Ellen and Mae, Honor and me. But it was a terrible thing to lose the girls and especially Dara, because you must understand, this was not the first time. When Dara was one year old we stood in the same place, watching her and her mother, our sister Caer, leave. And now, by choice, we had sent her and her sisters away. We were losing again.

...

Making my way to the gate I thought how quickly the years had come in. In many ways, it seemed only yesterday my sisters Honor, Caer, and I had been the young ones. Sometimes I'd forget Caer had been gone from the mountain for twenty-six years and had been dead eighteen years. Honor and I were 'the aunts' now. Not the *old* aunts, perhaps, but at this rate it wouldn't be long.

Twenty-six years since Caer had left with baby Dara. She was the first Cleary woman in living memory to leave this place. We knew we'd never see our sister again, but we understood she had to go. We, Honor and I, stayed on at our mountain home, minding the farm and the people as the women of our family have done for generations.

We are *Bean Feasa*, wise women, healers, or witches. It depends on what you need, it depends on who you talk to. People travel from across the country, even from out in the world for our help. Charms, cures, curses, though we don't deal in curses now, that's in the past.

...

Caer left with a man who'd come from Cádiz in Spain out of interest for a book he was writing on the healing traditions of Europe. Marius had the openness and sensitivity of an artist, one of those rare people you don't meet very often, secure in his own skin, a free spirit. He saw in her eyes the destruction and pain and found he wasn't afraid and wouldn't break himself against it. From the first moment he saw her he knew he'd never love again.

At the time Honor said, 'Caer has all the luck.'

We were working in the garden. There'd been a glut of crops that year and it took a lot of saving. Our backs were sore, our baskets heaving.

'You can't be serious?'

'I'm only serious about the fact she gets two great loves, and gets away from here.'

'Three great loves,' I said. 'You forget Dara, Dara makes it worthwhile for all of us.'

'I know, but I can't help it. Look at him, he's beautiful, he's crazy about her. I envy her escape.'

'Even so, how can she do it? How can she leave us?'

A pained look passed over her face. 'I don't know,' she said. 'Strength I suppose. She's been through the fires but she's still strong.'

'Yes, yes, I know,' I muttered, kicking over a basket. 'Stronger than our mother was, stronger than we are. How often did we hear that growing up?'

'You're worried about the quest? Of what will become of us *weaklings* without her?'

'I know life goes on but her time on the quest is done, a *Bean Feasa* can't practice with pain in her heart, you know this.'

'I seem to manage.'

'You're only bitter, it's hardly the same!' We laughed at that.

'What about the child? I mean, she will come back one day, won't she?'

Honor nodded. 'One day.'

'So is there nothing we can do now except wait? Rot?'

'Waiting is so long... I wouldn't say *nothing*.'

She had a flair for mystery and I wasn't satisfied yet. I wanted assurance, something. I wanted her to tell me that our time wasn't done, our chances gone. After all, it mattered more to her than it did to me, but I was just as bound as she was. Would *she* take the quest now? Could she? Did I even want her to?

I pushed her.

'Well that tells me a lot, Honor. The quest abandoned, and after everything we did. You're not forgetting?'

'*Forget?*' she snapped glacially. 'How could I forget?'

We worked on then, seeking solace in the black earth, peace for the peace-less. You could find it there sometimes, but forget? You could never forget. I was sorry I'd said it. In truth, I was more content here than she was. This fate, it wasn't so difficult for me. Our sister's laughter came to us in waves, languorous as the air itself.

'Maybe she can make it,' I suggested. I meant it as encouragement, as hope.

But without pause she replied, '*My envy of escape and love are foolish, for strong or not there'll be no escape for her, and maybe no escape for us.*'

'Why? What have you seen?'

'I've seen nothing. It's too hot now, I'm going in.'

Honor hadn't seen a future for our sister, though at the time she didn't tell me, and yet, for all of that still she envied her.

Follow Jane

Facebook: www.facebook.com/thatcuriousloveofgreen

Instagram: @janegilheaneybarry

Sign up to Jane's mailing list at:

https://mailchi.mp/b609c2263737/janegilheaneybarry

Support the work at Patreon:

https://www.patreon.com/janegilheaneybarry

For workshops and press: janebarry17@gmail.com

Thank you for reading

I hope you have enjoyed this book. If you can be persuaded to write a reader review on Amazon I'd really appreciate it.

Reviews on Amazon are critical to the success of an author these days.

Sign up to Jane's mailing list at:
https://mailchi.mp/b609c2263737/janegilheaneybarry

48300242R00089

Printed in Poland
by Amazon Fulfillment
Poland Sp. z o.o., Wrocław